Science

PRACTICE QUESTIONS

Pauline Hannigan

The Publishers would like to thank the following for permission to reproduce copyright material.

Photo credits
Page 14 left © jclegg; page 14 right © Quasarphoto; page 17 © T.OTSUKA; page 39 © cjp

Acknowledgements

Rising Stars is grateful to the following schools who will be utilising Achieve to prepare their students for the National Tests: Chacewater Community Primary School, Cornwall; Coppice Primary School, Essex; Edgewood Primary School, Notts; Henwick Primary School, Eltham; Norwood Primary School, Southport; Sacred Heart Catholic Primary School, Manchester; Sunnyfields Primary School, Hendon; Tennyson Road Primary School, Luton.

Every effort has been made to trace all copyright holders, but if any have been inadvertently overlooked, the Publishers will be pleased to make the necessary arrangements at the first opportunity.

Although every effort has been made to ensure that website addresses are correct at time of going to press, Rising Stars cannot be held responsible for the content of any website mentioned in this book. It is sometimes possible to find a relocated web page by typing in the address of the home page for a website in the URL window of your browser.

Hachette UK's policy is to use papers that are natural, renewable and recyclable products and made from wood grown in sustainable forests. The logging and manufacturing processes are expected to conform to the environmental regulations of the country of origin.

ISBN: 978 1 78339 554 5

© Rising Stars UK Ltd 2015

First published in 2015 by Rising Stars UK Ltd, part of Hodder Education, an Hachette UK Company

Carmelite House

50 Victoria Embankment

London EC4Y 0DZ

www.risingstars-uk.com

Author: Pauline Hannigan

Series Editor: Ed Walsh

Educational Consultant: Shan Oswald

Accessibility Reviewer: Vivien Kilburn

Publishers: Kate Jamieson and Gillian Lindsey

Project Manager: Debbie Allen

Editorial: Jo Murray, Lynette Woodward, John Durkin, Fiona Leonard

Cover design: Burville-Riley Partnership

Illustrations by John Storey, Pen and Ink Book Co Ltd

Text design and typeset by the Pen and Ink Book Co Ltd

Printed by the Gutenberg Press, Malta

A catalogue record for this title is available from the British Library.

Contents

Welcome to Achieve Key Stage 2 Science Practice Questions 100+

In this book you will find lots of practice and information to help you be successful in the Key Stage 2 Science sampling tests. You will look again at some of the same key knowledge that was in Achieve 100, but you will use it to tackle trickier questions and apply it in more complex ways.

About the Key Stage 2 Science National Sampling Tests

Not all schools sit the Science sampling tests; a selection is chosen to use them. The tests will take place in the summer term in Year 6. They will be done in your school and will be marked by examiners – not by your teacher.

The tests are divided into three papers:

Paper b: Biology – 25 minutes (22 marks)
Paper c: Chemistry – 25 minutes (22 marks)
Paper p: Physics – 25 minutes (22 marks)

- In each test, there will be a mixture of question types, including multiple-choice, labelling diagrams, short responses such as one or two words, or longer responses where you need to describe an experiment or explain your answer.
- The number of marks will vary depending on how difficult the question is.
- Between 25 and 35 per cent of the questions will test your ability to 'work scientifically'. This means using your scientific understanding to plan or analyse investigations.

Test techniques

Before the tests

- Try to revise little and often, rather than in long sessions.
- Choose a time of day when you are not tired or hungry.
- Choose somewhere quiet so you can focus.
- Revise with a friend. You can encourage and learn from each other.
- Read the 'Top tips' throughout this book to remind you of important points in answering test questions.

During the tests

- READ THE QUESTION AND READ IT AGAIN.
- If you find a question difficult to answer, move on; you can always come back to it later.
- Always answer a multiple-choice question. If you really can't work out the answer, have a guess.
- Check to see how many marks a question is worth. Have you written enough to 'earn' those marks in your answer?
- Read the question again after you have answered it. Make sure you have given the correct number of answers within a question, e.g. 'Tick **two** boxes'.
- If you have any time left at the end, go back to the questions you have missed. If you really do not know the answers, make guesses.

Where to get help:

- Pages 6–21 practise Biology.
- Pages 22–33 practise Chemistry.
- Pages 34–51 practise Physics.
- Pages 53–56 provide the answers.

Health and digestion

To achieve 100+ you need to:
* explain why animals, including humans, need the right types of nutrition from their food
* explain the function of parts of the **digestive system**
* explain how diet, exercise, drugs and lifestyle can affect our bodies
* explain how **nutrients** and water move around the body.

1 Tick **all** the boxes that show how smoking can have a bad effect on the body.

Make you cough. ☐

Give you stomach ache. ☐

Cause lung cancer. ☐

Make your hair fall out. ☐

Stain your teeth. ☐

Cause heart disease. ☐

☐ 1

(1 mark)

2 Sugar is a good source of energy. However, it is important not to eat too many sugary foods. Complete the sentences below by writing the correct words on the answer lines.

Eating too many sugary foods can make _____

_____ .

Too much sugar can affect your teeth by _____

_____ .

☐ 2

(1 mark)

3 Glucose is a simple sugar that doesn't need digesting. Runners often take glucose tablets because it gets into the blood very quickly as a quick source of energy.

Explain how the glucose from the tablet reaches the muscles in a runner's legs.

_____

_____

☐ 3

(1 mark)

! Top tip
* Think about how food travels through the digestive system from when it is put in the mouth.

/ 3

Total for this page

4 The class made a model of the digestive system.

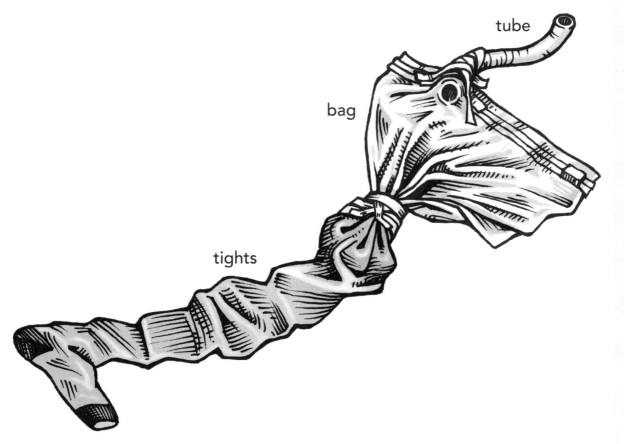

Explain what each part of the model represents and describe what happens there.

tube

_____

bag

_____

tights

_____

Food chains

To achieve 100+ you need to:
* ★ draw and interpret a **food chain**
* ★ explain how **consumers, producers, predators** and **prey** fit into a food chain.

1 Plants and animals can play different parts in a food chain. Tick the **correct boxes** in the table to show whether each plant or animal is a producer, prey or predator in a food chain. You can tick more than one box for each plant or animal.

1

(2 marks)

Plant or animal	Producer	Prey	Predator
1. grass			
2. owl			
3. caterpillar			
4. rabbit			
5. oak tree			
6. fox			
7. hawk			
8. slug			
9. thrush			
10. lettuce			

2 a) Choose **four** of the animals and plants above to make a food chain. Write the name of **one** plant or animal in each box below.

2a

(1 mark)

b) What do the arrows show?

_____

2b

(1 mark)

c) What do all food chains have in common?

_____

2c

(1 mark)

d) Why do most food chains only contain a few plants or animals?

_____

2d

(1 mark)

/ 6

Total for this page

3 The picture shows several food chains, which together make up a food web.

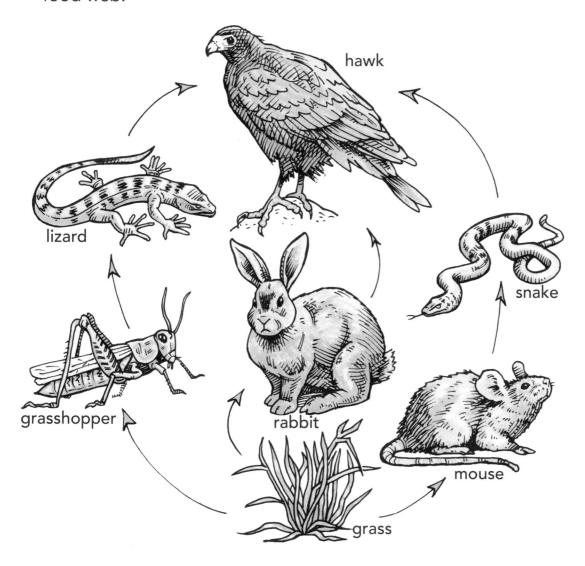

a) Explain why the hawk is the top predator.

_____

3a

(1 mark)

b) One year there were no grasshoppers. What effect could this have on each of the other animals in the food web?

3b

(2 marks)

lizard _____

hawk _____

rabbit _____

mouse _____

snake _____

!Top tip

• An animal can be a predator but also be prey for another predator higher up the food chain.

/ 3

Heart and circulation

To achieve 100+ you need to:
* identify the main parts of the human **circulatory system** and explain their function
* explain how the circulatary system works.

1 Blood travels round the body. Starting at the lungs, put the parts of the circulatory system in order.

1

(1 mark)

vein   capillary   heart   other parts of body   artery

1 lungs	2	3	4

5	6

2 Blood carries oxygen around our bodies.

2

(1 mark)

Complete the sentences below by writing the correct words on the answer lines.

Oxygenated blood travels from the lungs to the

_____.

Then it goes _____.

/2

Total for
this page

3   The children are investigating the effect of exercise on their pulse rates. They draw a table of their results.

	Pulse rate per minute		
	Before star jumps	Straight after 100 star jumps	After resting for 5 minutes
Child A	98	135	99
Child B	96	130	94
Child C	88	123	90
Child D	90	137	95

a) What **pattern** do you notice in their results?

_____

_____

3a

(1 mark)

b) What is happening in their bodies that explains why they get these results?

_____

_____

3b

(1 mark)

c) Sometimes you have to repeat results in an investigation. Do you think that the children need to repeat these results? Why?

_____

_____

3c

(1 mark)

d) Why do all the children not have the same pulse rate at the start?

_____

_____

3d

(1 mark)

e) How do you think the results might be different for:

i) someone who does a lot of PE?

_____

ii) someone who eats an unhealthy diet?

_____

3e

(1 mark)

Top tip

- Compare how the results for each child go up and down to find a pattern in the results.

/ 5

Classification and keys

To achieve 100+ you need to:

★ explain how living things are grouped in the **classification system**
★ use and make **keys** to help group, identify and name some living things
★ explain why scientists need to group plants and animals
★ describe some of the differences between **mammals, amphibians, reptiles, fish, insects** and **birds**.

1 Microorganisms are one group of living things. This group can be divided again into three main groups. One group is viruses. Give the names of the **other two** groups.

1. _____

2. _____

(2 marks)

2 Sometimes keys are used to identify living things. Tick **all** the questions that would be useful for making a key about the animals in a zoo.

Does it have more than four legs? ☐

Is it big? ☐

Does it have fins? ☐

Does it have fingers? ☐

Is it fat? ☐

(1 mark)

3 a) Write a question in box A and in box B that would sort these animals.

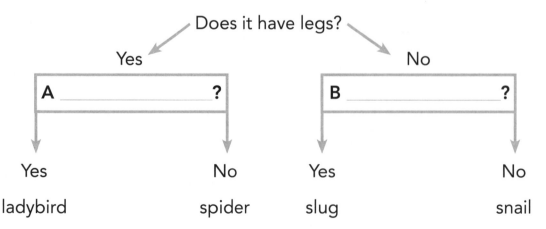

(1 mark)

b) All of these animals belong to a group of animals called

_____.

(1 mark)

/5

Total for this page

4 Write a difference between each of pair of animal groups.

4

(1 mark)

Animal groups	Difference between them
Birds and mammals	
Reptiles and amphibians	
Fish and amphibians	

!Top tip

- Sometimes animals in different classification groups share some characteristics.

/1

Total for
this page   13

Inheritance

To achieve 100+ you need to:
* ★ identify how living things vary in appearance compared to their parents
* ★ distinguish between **inherited** and environmental features.

1 Some features are inherited from parents and some are as a result of things in the environment; sometimes they are due to both. **Match** each feature to the correct word.

colour of eyes

weight

colour of skin

length of hair

shape of chin

inherited

both

caused by environment

2 A Labradoodle is a kind of dog. One parent is a labrador and the other parent is a poodle.

golden labrador   standard poodle

The puppies from these two parents may look different. Describe **two** different ways they may look.

1. _____

2. _____

3 a) Identical twins develop from a single fertilised egg that splits early in its development. Explain why both twins look the same.

3a

(1 mark)

_____

_____

_____

   b) Describe **one** thing the twins could do to make them look different.

3b

(1 mark)

_____

_____

_____

4 One piglet in a litter of ten is much smaller than the others. Give **one** possible reason for this.

4

(1 mark)

_____

Adaptation and change

To achieve 100+ you need to:
* ★ relate **adaptations** of living things to their environment
* ★ recognise that these adaptations may lead to **evolutionary change**
* ★ identify how **environmental change** may be a threat to the survival of living things.

The class is finding out about birds.

1 They find out that Charles Darwin was a scientist who studied finches and discovered that their beaks were adapted to the food they ate.

1
(1 mark)

The children look at the beaks of other birds and agree with Darwin. **Match** each bird to the food it eats.

Bird   **Food**

kestrel   mice

heron   insects

warbler   fish

2 The children are finding out about a bird called a crossbill that has a beak that is adapted to eat seeds from inside pine cones.

2
(1 mark)

What do you think would happen to the crossbills if the pine forest where they live is cleared for a housing development?

/ 2

Total for
this page

3 The children are finding out about a seabird called a cormorant. Cormorants dive under the water and catch fish. They have long beaks and webbed feet.

a) Explain how the features of a cormorant help it survive in its environment.

 3a

(1 mark)

_____

_____

_____

b) How might the features of the cormorant adapt further in the future so it becomes even better at catching fish?

3b

(1 mark)

_____

_____

_____

! Top tip
• Adaptations are often concerned with finding food.

/ 2

Total for
this page   17

Investigating plants

To achieve 100+ you need to:
* ★ relate the parts of plants to their functions
* ★ investigate what plants need to live and grow.

1 Write **true** or **false** for each statement about plants.

True or **false**?

Plants grow tall in dark areas. ....

Only water is taken in by the roots. ....

The stem contains tubes. ....

Plants cannot grow in shady places. ....

Plants must have air to live. ....

<table>
<tr><td></td><td>1</td></tr>
<tr><td>(2 marks)</td><td></td></tr>
</table>

2 Jack is growing some beans in a jar so he can see how they grow.

Jack puts some damp tissue paper into a jar and plants a bean in it. After a few days the beans begin to grow. After a week the first leaves show.

a) What is the name for the process when a seed starts to grow?

....

<table>
<tr><td></td><td>2a</td></tr>
<tr><td>(1 mark)</td><td></td></tr>
</table>

b) How does the water travel from the jar into the leaves?

....

<table>
<tr><td></td><td>2b</td></tr>
<tr><td>(1 mark)</td><td></td></tr>
<tr><td></td><td>/ 4</td></tr>
<tr><td colspan="2">Total for this page</td></tr>
</table>

3 Jack wants to know if a plant can survive without roots. He sets up an investigation using three different bean plants. He cuts all the roots off plant A. He cuts half of the roots off plant B. He deos not cut any roots off plant C.

a) How could Jack improve his plan?

_____

_____

3a

(1 mark)

b) Jack measures each plant and then puts them on the window sill. He adds more water when the tissue paper feels dry. After another week he measures each plant again and records what it looks like. He puts his results in the table below.

3b

(1 mark)

Plant	Height after 1 week (in cm)	Height after 2 weeks (in cm)	Appearance
A	6	6.0	Leaves have shrivelled.
B	5	6.5	Leaves look healthy.
C	6	9.5	Leaves look healthy. New leaves have appeared.

Explain the difference in the results using what you know about plants.

_____

_____

_____

c) Suggest a further question that Jack might want to investigate because of these results.

_____

_____

3c

(1 mark)

 Top tip

• Plants are living things so you cannot always rely on the results of tests that you do on them.

/ 3

Total for this page

The life cycle of flowering plants

To achieve 100+ you need to:
★ explain how flowering flowers **reproduce**, including the function of different parts of the flower and the processes of **pollination**, seed formation and **seed dispersal**.

1   Tick the boxes that show the female parts of a flower.

Tick **two**.

stamen   ☐

pollen   ☐

ovule   ☐

anther   ☐

stigma   ☐

☐ 1

(1 mark)

2   Write the correct words on the lines below to show part of the life cycle of a flowering plant.

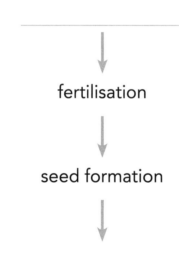

_____

↓

fertilisation

↓

seed formation

↓

_____

☐ 2

(2 marks)

/ 3

Total for this page

3 Explain how each of these two different seeds might get carried a very long way from its parent plant.

a) a cocklebur

3a

(1 mark)

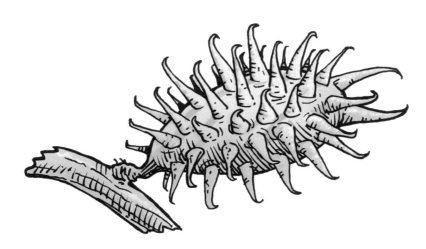

_____

b) a sycamore

3b

(1 mark)

_____

4 What might happen if the seeds started to grow near the parent plant?

4

(1 mark)

_____

_____

 Top tip

• The appearance of a seed can give a clue as to how it is carried away from the parent plant.

/ 3

Total for
this page

21

Fossils

To achieve 100+ you need to:
* explain how **fossils** are formed
* explain how some living things have changed over time.

1 Write **true** or **false** for each statement about fossils.

True or **false**?

1

(2 marks)

Fossils can be made of minerals or rock. _____

Fossils are always made from the hard
parts of animals. _____

There are only fossils of plants and animals
that are extinct. _____

Fossils are still being formed today. _____

2 Complete the sentences below by writing the correct words on
the answer lines.

2

(1 mark)

Lots of plants and animals _____ before they are
buried and so do not become fossils.

When dead plants or animals are in places like _____
it is easy for them to be buried.

3 Explain **two** things that fossils **cannot** tell us about animals that
were on Earth millions of years ago.

3

(1 mark)

1. _____

2. _____

> **! Top tip**
> * The soft parts of an animal do not usually become fossils.

/4

*Total for
this page*

4

This fossil of a footprint is known as a trace fossil. It shows the activity of the animal rather than being the remains of its body. It was formed when the animal walked across some wet mud.

a) What do you think happened next so that the footprint eventually became a fossil?

4a

(1 mark)

b) What would this fossil show about the dinosaur that would not be shown by finding fossilised bones?

4b

(1 mark)

c) Think of a different type of trace fossil that could show the behaviour of an animal.

4c

(1 mark)

/3

Solids, liquids and gases

To achieve 100+ you need to:
* ★ decide if materials are **solids**, **liquids** or **gases** and say why
* ★ identify materials that do not fit into solid, liquid or gas groups
* ★ explain how some materials change **state** when they are heated or cooled.

1   A solid, a liquid and a gas show different properties. **Match** each word to the correct property. You can use more than one property.

☐ 1

(2 marks)

solid

liquid

gas

is easily squashed

holds its shape

changes shape depending on the container

can be cut or shaped

fills any container it is in

can be poured

2   Complete the sentences below by writing the correct answer on the answer lines.

☐ 2

(1 mark)

The name of the process when a liquid changes to a gas is

_____.

The name of the process when a gas changes to a liquid is

_____.

3   At what temperature does water change from a liquid to a gas?

☐ 3

(1 mark)

_____

☐ / 4

Total for this page

4 Sara is making some ice cream by mixing milk, cream and sugar. She knows she can make it freeze by putting it in a bag inside a bag of ice and salt and then shaking it. She isn't sure how much salt to put in the ice so she decides to try different amounts to see if it makes a difference to the time it takes for the ice cream to freeze. She makes a table of her results.

Number of spoons of salt	Time taken for ice cream to freeze (mins)
6	20
8	
10	12
12	10

a) Fill in the box to show how long it takes for the ice cream to freeze with 8 spoons of salt in the ice.

4a

(1 mark)

b) What conclusion could Sara make about how different amounts of salt affect how quickly the ice cream freezes?

4b

(1 mark)

c) What sort of change happens as the ice cream freezes?

4c

(1 mark)

5 Iron is a solid and a metal.

a) Explain how iron could be changed from a solid to a liquid.

5a

(1 mark)

b) Explain why you would not be able to do this change at home.

5b

(1 mark)

Top tip
- Different materials change state at different temperatures.

/5

Total for this page

25

The water cycle

To achieve 100+ you need to:
* identify the various stages in the **water cycle** and explain how these relate to processes such as **evaporation** and **condensation**
* explain how temperature affects the rate at which water evaporates.

1 Write the words below in the correct order to show the way that water travels in the water cycle. One has been done for you.

condenses   returns to rivers and seas   forms clouds

falls to the Earth's surface   cools

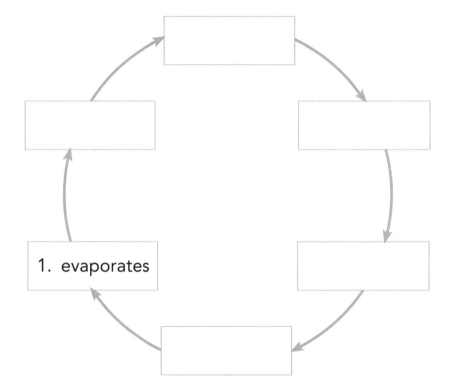

1. evaporates

2 Name **three** different ways that water can return to the Earth's surface.

1. _____

2. _____

3. _____

/ 2

Total for this page

3 The class is investigating whether the size of the surface area of a container affects how quickly the water evaporates.

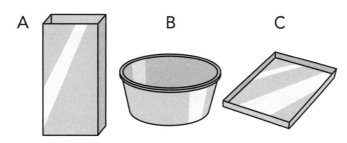

A   B   C

They use three containers. They put 100 ml of water in each container and put them outside. After two days they measure the volume of water in each container again. They record the results in a table.

Container	Amount left in container after two days
A	95 ml
B	15 ml
C	50 ml

a) Draw a graph of their results.

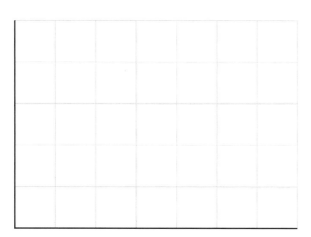

3a
(1 mark)

b) What conclusion could the class make about how the size of the surface area affects how quickly water evaporates?

3b
(1 mark)

_____

c) Use your scientific knowledge to explain why this is so.

3c
(1 mark)

_____

_____

 Top tip

• Look for a pattern in the results between the things you are comparing to help you draw a conclusion.

/ 3

Total for this page   27

Reversible changes

To achieve 100+ you need to:
* explain how the idea of **reversible changes** can be applied to **dissolving** and mixing
* explain how a **solution** is made and what it consists of
* explain how a solid can be retrieved from a solution and from a **mixture**
* apply ideas about different types of materials to suggest how they can be separated.

1 Write **true** or **false** for each statement about dissolving.

	True or **false**?
You can make a material dissolve quicker by stirring.	
When a material dissolves in a liquid it makes a solution.	
Dissolving is a reversible change.	
Solutions are always colourless.	
If a material dissolves you can dissolve any amount of it in the liquid.	

1

(2 marks)

2 The class is investigating how the grain size of sugar affects how quickly it dissolves. They record their results in a table.

Size of sugar grains	Time taken to dissolve (in seconds)		
	1st try	2nd try	3rd try
Small	18	24	22
Medium	38	35	42
Large	69	60	59

a) What equipment could they use to do their investigation?

2a

(1 mark)

b) What things do they need to keep the same?

2b

(1 mark)

/ 4

Total for this page

c) Why do they repeat their tests?

2c

(1 mark)

d) Use the table to explain how grain size affects the time it takes for the sugar to dissolve.

2d

(1 mark)

3 The children are given a challenge by their teacher. He gives them a mixture of salt, flour and iron filings in water. He asks them to separate the mixture. Explain how they can get the three materials back.

3

(2 marks)

! Top tip

• Sometimes you need to use more than one process to separate materials.

/ 4

Total for this page

Irreversible changes

To achieve 100+ you need to:
★ explain that some changes are **irreversible** (non-reversible).

1 Tick the statement that is true only for an irreversible change.

Tick **one.**

New materials are formed. ☐

Heat is produced. ☐

You can never get the original materials back. ☐

A gas is produced. ☐

You have to heat the mixture. ☐

2 When a candle burns some of the wax changes to liquid and then a gas. Complete the sentence below.

Burning a candle is an irreversible change because

_____

_____.

3 Explain why a nail rusting is an irreversible change.

_____

_____

4 Complete the following sentence:

When you mix bicarbonate of soda with vinegar, lots of bubbles

of _____ are formed. You cannot get

the bicarbonate of soda or _____ back

again so this is _____ change.

5 The children test some different materials. They want to see how the materials change when the materials are heated and then cooled again. They record their results in a table.

a) Complete the final column of the table to show what sort of change happens to each material. Write **reversible** or **irreversible** in each box.

5a
(2 marks)

Material	What happens when it is heated	What happens when it is cooled again	Reversible or irreversible change?
Solid butter	Turns to liquid	Turns to solid	
Raw beaten egg	Goes solid	It does not change	
Cake mixture (butter, sugar and egg mixed together)	The mixture gets bigger and the texture changes	It does not change	

b) Suggest another material they could test. Complete the final row of the table using this material.

5b
(1 mark)

Top tip

• An irreversible change is permanent.

/3

Total for this page

31

Properties and uses of materials

To achieve 100+ you need to:
* ★ explain how **properties** of materials can be used to group them
* ★ explain how the properties of materials can be tested
* ★ justify uses of materials with reference to their properties.

Ben is going to make a hat for the winter.

1   First he needs to choose a suitable fabric to use. Tick **three** properties that would **not** be useful for a hat.

(1 mark)

Tick **three**.

waterproof   ☐

absorbent   ☐

stretchy   ☐

rigid   ☐

transparent   ☐

2   Ben decides to test some fabrics to see which would keep him warmest. He wraps a cup of hot water in each of the fabrics. He puts a thermometer in each cup of hot water and records the temperature. After an hour he takes the temperature of the water in each cup again.

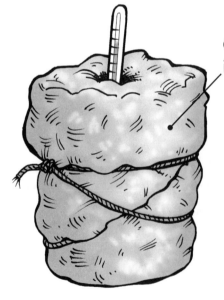

Glass jar wrapped in fleece

/1

Total for this page

Ben records his results in the table below.

Type of fabric	Temperature at start (°C)	Temperature after one hour (°C)	Difference in temperature (°C)
Felt	80	65	
Fleece	79	58	
Wool	77	52	

a) Fill in the final column in the table.

2a

(1 mark)

b) Ben decides the fleece will keep him warmest. Explain if he is right.

2b

(1 mark)

3 Suggest how Ben could improve his test.

3

(1 mark)

4 Describe how Ben could investigate a different property before choosing the fabric for his hat.

4

(1 mark)

Top tip

- Decide what you think the results show first. Then compare this with a conclusion you have been given.

/ 4

Conductors and switches

To achieve 100+ you need to:

★ explain how **switches** affect the way a circuit works
★ identify some common **conductors** and **insulators**
★ give examples of where we use insulators and conductors in everyday life
★ draw a range of **circuit diagrams** using the correct symbols.

1 Decide whether these statements about switches are **true** or **false**. Write **true** or **false** for each statement.

(2 marks)

True or **false**?

A switch can be used to complete a circuit. _____

A switch can be used to break a circuit. _____

Switches can be made completely from plastic. _____

It doesn't matter where you put a switch in a simple circuit. _____

A light switch has a plastic cover because plastic conducts electricity. _____

2 Give an example of when a 'push and hold' switch is used and explain why it is used then.

(1 mark)

_____

_____

/3

Total for this page

3 Toby makes the circuit shown in the diagram below. He makes switch A from a metal paperclip and switch B from a plastic straw.

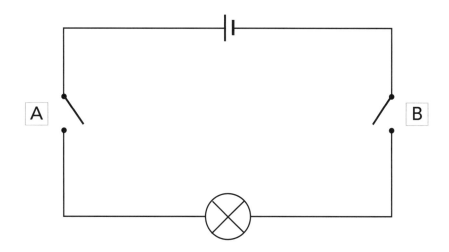

Toby thinks that the bulb will glow when he closes switch A and switch B. Explain whether you agree with Toby by completing the sentence below.

When Toby closes switch A and switch B the bulb will

_____

because _____ .

 Top tip

- Sometimes a complete circuit is only needed for a short while and this is usually controlled by a special type of switch.

/1

Changing circuits

To achieve 100+ you need to:
★ explain why the number of **cells** affects how components work in a circuit.

1   a)   **Draw** a circuit diagram in the box below of a simple circuit with one bulb, two cells and a switch.

1a

(1 mark)

     b)   Tick the statements that show how to make the bulb glow brighter.

1b

(1 mark)

Turn the cells around. ☐

Take the switch out. ☐

Add another cell. ☐

Add another bulb. ☐

Take a cell away. ☐

2   Bella makes a toy roundabout. She constructs a simple circuit to make the roundabout spin around.

2

(1 mark)

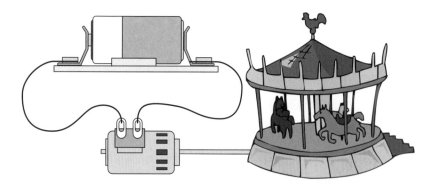

Bella draws a circuit diagram of the circuit she made. What symbol should she use to represent the motor? Draw the symbol in the box below.

! Top tip

* The way that some components work depends on how they are put in the circuit.

/3

Total for
this page

3 a) Explain how Bella could make her roundabout go faster.

_____

3a

(1 mark)

b) How could she test her idea?

_____

3b

(1 mark)

c) How could Bella make the roundabout spin the other way?

_____

3c

(1 mark)

4 The class is investigating whether using a longer piece of wire in a circuit affects the brightness of a bulb. They change the length of the wire between the bulb and the cell and use a datalogger to measure the brightness of the bulb. The readings it shows are measured in lux. They record their results in a table.

Length of wire (cm)	Brightness of bulb (lux)
25	382
50	326
75	275
100	

a) Complete the table by recording in the empty box how bright you think the bulb might be.

b) Use the table to draw a line graph of their results.

c) What conclusion can the children draw from their results? What evidence helps them to decide?

_____

_____

Gravity and resistance

To achieve 100+ you need to:

★ explain that **gravity** is a **non-contact force** that attracts objects towards Earth

★ explain how movement may be affected by **friction** or **resistance** from air or water.

1   Solids experience different types of forces. **Match** each description of a solid to the name of the force acting on it.

When two solids rub together	water resistance
When a solid falls to the ground	friction
When a solid moves through air	gravity
When a solid moves through a liquid	air resistance

1
(1 mark)

2   The class is testing the weight of different objects in air and in water. They make a table of their results.

Object	Weight in air	Weight in water
mug	4.5	3.7
book	8.5	6.5
shoe	9.0	7.3
scissors	5.0	
stone	10.5	

a) Suggest what the missing measurements might be, adding them in the table. Add the units to the table.

2a
(1 mark)

b) What instrument might they use?

_____

2b
(1 mark)

c) Explain why the objects seem to **weigh less** in water than they do in air.

_____

_____

2c
(1 mark)

! Top tip

• Think about all the forces that are acting on the objects.

/ 4

Total for this page

3

a) Name **three** forces that are acting on the girl as she rides her bicycle.

3a

(*1 mark*)

1. _____

2. _____

3. _____

b) Describe **one** thing she could do to reduce one of these forces.

3b

(*1 mark*)

/ 2

Mechanisms

To achieve 100+ you need to:

★ explain how the size and direction of the force needed to move something can be changed by a simple machine.

1 Write **true** or **false** for each statement.

True or **false**?

A lever can use a small amount of force to lift a heavier weight.

_____

If you use two pulleys to lift an object, you need to use twice as much force.

_____

Gears can be used to change the direction of something that is rotating.

_____

Gears have cogs.

_____

A seesaw does not have a pivot point.

_____

1

(2 marks)

2 Cranes are used to lift and move heavy loads.

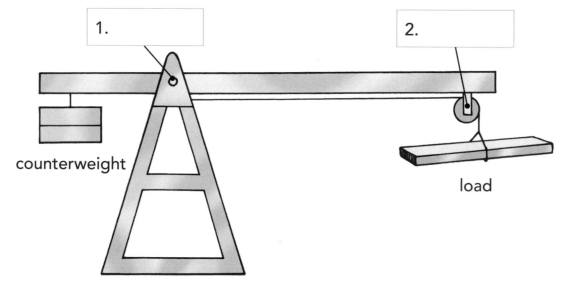

1.

2.

counterweight

load

a) Label the **two** parts of the crane. Write the names in the boxes.

b) A crane needs a counterweight so _____

_____.

2a

(2 marks)

2b

(1 mark)

/5

Total for this page

3 Genna has some balance scales.

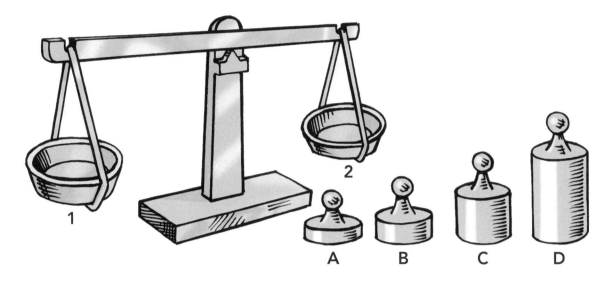

a) Genna puts mass A in pan 1 and masses B, C and D in pan 2. Which pan will go down?

3a

(1 mark)

b) How can Genna make the pans balance without adding anything to or taking anything out of either pan?

3b

(1 mark)

/ 2

Total for
this page 41

How we see

To achieve 100+ you need to:
* ★ explain how we need light to see things
* ★ use a diagram to explain how light is **reflected** from surfaces.

1 We need light to be able to see. All of the statements below are true. Tick the **only** statement that describes how we see an object.

<table>
<tr><td></td><td>1</td></tr>
<tr><td></td><td>(1 mark)</td></tr>
</table>

Tick **one**.

Light travels in straight lines in all directions. ☐

Light is blocked by opaque materials. ☐

We see shiny surfaces better than dull ones because they reflect more light. ☐

Light travels from the light source, bounces off the object and then goes into our eyes. ☐

Our eyes adjust to total darkness and then we can see. ☐

2 Sam has a reflector on the back of his bike.

<table>
<tr><td></td><td>2</td></tr>
<tr><td></td><td>(1 mark)</td></tr>
</table>

Complete the sentence below by writing the correct words on the answer lines.

The reflector does not need batteries because _____

_____ .

/2

Total for this page

3 Sometimes there is a mirror at the side of the road where there is a sharp bend to help motorists see what is coming.

a) Explain why we can't see round a corner.

 3a

_____

(1 mark)

b) Draw a diagram with arrows to show how a driver approaching the corner can use the mirror to see a car approaching the corner in the other direction.

 3b

(1 mark)

/ 2

Total for this page

Shadows

To achieve 100+ you need to:
* explain how **shadows** are formed and how the size of shadows may change.

The class is investigating shadows.

1   Write **true** or **false** for each statement about shadows.

True or **false**?

Only opaque objects make shadows.   _____

Translucent objects make shadows.   _____

All shadows are as dark as each other.   _____

Shadows move if the object making the shadow moves.   _____

The angle of the light source can affect the length of a shadow.   _____

1
(2 marks)

2   The children use a light projector to make shadow pictures of each other.

2
(1 mark)

Light travels in straight lines. Explain, with the help of a diagram, why this makes the shadows the same shape as the children's heads.

_____

_____

/3

Total for this page

3 The children use a light projector and a book to make shadows. They put the light projector one metre from the wall and do not move it. They put the book at different distances from the wall and measure the height of the shadow made by the book.

They record their results and then draw a graph.

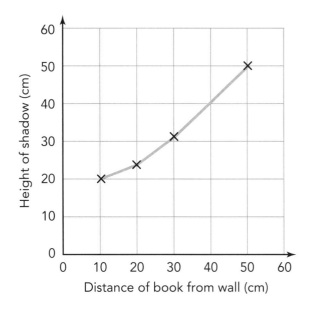

a) What is the height of the shadow when the book is 40 cm from the wall?

3a

(1 mark)

_____

b) Describe the relationship between the distance of the book from the wall and the height of the shadow.

3b

(1 mark)

_____

! Top tip

• Look for a pattern in the way both measurements change.

/2

Total for this page

Pitch and volume

To achieve 100+ you need to:
* explain how the features of an object could affect the **pitch**
* explain the link between the **volume** of a sound and the strength of the **vibrations**.

1 You can play high and low notes on a violin. A violin has six strings. Decide whether the following actions would make the note **higher** or **lower**.

	1
	(1 mark)

	Higher or **lower?**
Playing a thinner string	
Making the string looser	
Putting your finger on the string	
Playing a thicker string	
Making the string tighter	

2 Groups of children want to carry out an investigation to prove that sounds get fainter as they travel away.

a) Write down **one** way they could do this.

_____

	2a
	(1 mark)

b) Explain **one** reason why different groups might get different results.

_____

_____

	2b
	(1 mark)

/3

Total for this page

3 Jan makes a water xylophone.

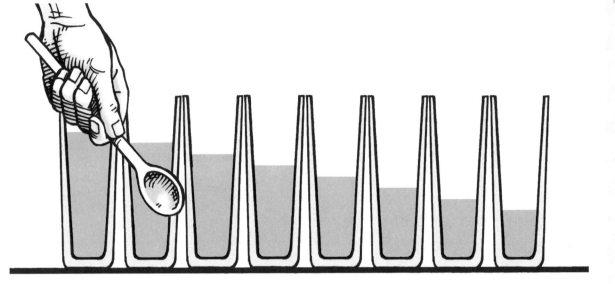

Describe the pattern she notices when she taps the glasses.

_____

_____

4 A tuning fork produces a particular note when it is struck.

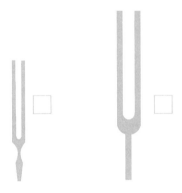

a) Tick the box next to the tuning fork that will have the highest pitch.

4a

(1 mark)

b) Explain your answer.

4b

(1 mark)

_____

_____

!` Top tip

• The less there is to vibrate, the higher the note.

/ 3

Our Solar System

To achieve 100+ you need to:
* recognise that the **Sun**, **Earth** and **Moon** are spheres
* explain how the Earth and other planets in our **Solar System** move round the Sun
* explain how the Moon moves round the Earth.

1 Write **true** or **false** for each statement about the Solar System.

True or **false**?

1
(2 marks)

The Solar System is made up of the Sun and all the stars in our galaxy. _____

The planets orbit the Sun in the same direction. _____

The Earth orbits the Sun. _____

The Moon travels around the Earth once in 24 hours. _____

It takes 356 days for the Earth to orbit the Sun. _____

2 The class is learning about the Solar System. They make a table showing some differences between the planets.

2
(1 mark)

Name of planet	Distance from the Sun (millions of km)	Time taken for one complete orbit of the Sun
Mercury	58	88 days
Venus	108	225 days
Earth	150	365 days
Mars	228	687 days
Jupiter	778	12 years
Saturn	1427	29 years
Uranus	2871	84 years
Neptune	4497	165 years

/ 3

Total for this page

What can the children say about how the time it takes for a planet to orbit the Sun changes with the distance it is from the Sun?

_____

_____

3   The class keeps a Moon diary. They draw pictures of how the Moon looks every day. They start their diary when it is a full Moon.

a)   How long will it be before there is another full Moon?

_____

3a

(1 mark)

b)   Explain what they notice about the shape of the Moon every time it appears in the sky.

_____

3b

(1 mark)

4   Why might you find it difficult to make an accurate model of the Solar System?

4

(1 mark)

_____

_____

5   Sometimes you can see the planets in the night sky. Complete the sentence below to explain why.

5

(1 mark)

A planet does not give off _____ but we can see it

because _____

_____ .

Top tip

•   The Moon orbiting the Earth affects how it appears in the sky.

/ 4

Total for this page

49

Day and night

To achieve 100+ you need to:
* explain how the movement of the Earth and Sun causes both day and night, and the apparent motion of the Sun across the sky
* apply the idea that light travels in straight lines
* explain patterns in the way that shadows can be changed in size.

1 Tick the statement that describes why we have day and night.

Tick **one**.

The Earth's axis is an imaginary line going through the ☐
centre of the Earth from pole to pole.

The Earth spins on its axis. ☐

It takes the Earth 24 hours to spin on its axis. ☐

It takes the Earth 24 hours to orbit the Sun. ☐

We always have the same amount of darkness as daylight. ☐

☐ 1
(1 mark)

2 Complete the sentence below:

In the morning, the Sun first appears in the _____.

It gets _____ in the sky until the middle of the day

and then gets _____ again.

☐ 2
(1 mark)

3 Explain how the position of the Sun in the sky affects the length
of shadows.

☐ 3
(3 marks)

_____

_____

/5

*Total for
this page*

4 The children put a stick in the playground and measure the length of the shadows it makes at different times in the day. They make a graph of their results.

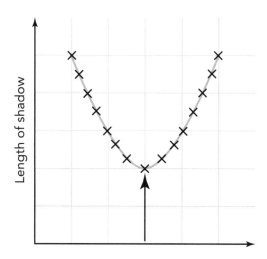

a) Label the x axis on the graph.

   What is missing off the y axis?

   _____

   4a

   (1 mark)

b) What time of the day is the arrow pointing to?

   _____

   4b

   (1 mark)

c) What is the graph showing about how the length of the shadows changes over the day?

   _____

   4c

   (1 mark)

 Top tip

• Shadows are formed when the light is blocked, so the position of the light source will affect the size of the shadows.

/3

Total for this page

Answers

All answers are worth 1 mark, unless otherwise indicated.

Health and digestion (pages 6–7)

1 tick: Make you cough; Cause lung cancer; Stain your teeth; Cause heart disease.
2 you overweight/obese; helping to make plaque, which can cause holes in the teeth enamel.
3 The glucose tablet is crushed by the teeth and swallowed and then travels to the small intestine. The nutrients pass from here into the blood, which then transports them to the muscles.
4 tube – oesophagus (transports food from mouth to stomach); bag – stomach (food is broken down into a liquid-like mixture); tights – intestine (nutrients/water is absorbed from here) (1 mark each)

Food chains (pages 8–9)

1 producer: 1, 5, 10
   prey: 3, 4, 8, 9
   predator: 2, 6, 7, 9
   (2 marks for all answers correct; 1 mark for 7–9 correct)
2 a)

grass/oak tree/lettuce	caterpillar/slug	thrush	fox/hawk

   b) The way the food/energy moves through the food chain.
   c) They all start with a plant/producer.
   d) Some energy is lost as it goes through the food chain and there would not be enough left for the last animal if the chain was too long; or animals often get larger as you move up the food chain.
3 a) The hawk is not eaten by any other animal.
   b) lizard: nothing to eat so would move away or die out
   hawk: fewer lizards to eat (so would be hungry or would eat more rabbits, mice and snakes)
   rabbit, mouse and snake: mouse and rabbit could increase because more grass to eat and if more mice you could get more snakes but could be eaten more by hawks (2 marks for all correct; 1 mark for four correct)

Heart and circulation (pages 10–11)

1 1 lungs; 2 heart; 3 artery; 4 capillary; 5 other parts of body; 6 vein
2 heart; around the body/to the body organs
3 a) The pulse rate goes up with exercise and then back to normal rate after 5 minutes. (1 mark – they need to mention both parts for the mark)
   b) The children's heart rates go up with exercise because the heart needs to pump more blood to their muscles to give them energy for the star jumps. The blood will be carrying the extra nutrients and oxygen to help the muscles work faster. Heart rate goes back to its normal rate when the muscles no longer have to work hard.
   c) To check if you have made a mistake in your readings.

It would be a good thing to do in this case.
   d) Children are all different and their hearts beat at different rates.
   e) i) has a slower heart rate at the beginning and/or has a smaller rise after star jumps.
      ii) has a faster heart rate at the beginning and/or a greater rise after star jumps.

Classification and keys (pages 12–13)

1 1. bacteria 2. fungi
2 tick: Does it have more than four legs?; Does it have fins?; Does it have fingers?
3 a) From the left: A Does it have six legs; or Can it fly? and B Does it have a shell?
   b) invertebrates
4 Birds and mammals: birds have feathers and lay eggs; mammals often have fur or hair, give birth to live young and feed their young on milk.
   Reptiles and amphibians: reptiles have rough or horny skins and usually lay eggs with leathery skins; amphibians have moist skins and breed and lay eggs in water.
   Fish and amphibians: fish have scales; amphibians have moist skins. (one difference identified for each pair for 1 mark)

Inheritance (pages 14–15)

1 inherited: colour of eyes, shape of chin; both: weight, colour of skin; caused by environment: length of hair (2 marks for all correct; 1 mark for four correct; if 'length of hair' is matched to both allow as this can be an inherited feature)
2 Colour of coat and whether coat is curly or smooth.
3 a) The egg splits after fertilisation so both twins come from a single egg from the mother and a single sperm from the father. So the features will be the same for each twin.
   b) e.g. cut/dye/curl hair; have a tattoo
4 It may be ill or have had less to eat than the others.

Adaptation and change (pages 16–17)

1 kestrel: mice; heron: fish; warbler: insects
2 They would find it difficult to eat; or they would find something different to eat; or they would fly away to a different area.
3 a) Their webbed feet help them swim fast under water; their beaks help them catch and hold onto fish.
   b) Its beak could become longer/sharper and its feet could become bigger.

Investigating plants (pages 18–19)

1 true: Plants grow tall in dark areas, The stem contains tubes, Plants must have air to live; false: Only water is taken in by the roots, Plants cannot grow in shady places (2 marks for all correct; 1 mark for four correct)
2 a) germination
   b) Through the roots and up the stem. (both must be included for 1 mark)

3 a) He could use more than one plant for each part of his investigation in case any died for a different reason.

b) Plant A is not getting any water so is beginning to die; plant B has grown a little and the leaves look healthy so must be getting some water to make food for the plant; plant C has grown most and has new leaves as it is getting plenty of water.

c) Questions to investigate could be: Is there a minimum number of roots a plants needs to survive?/Do all plants stop growing if they have no roots?

The life cycle of flowering plants (pages 20–21)

1 tick: ovule; stigma

2 pollination; (seed) dispersal

3 a) catch on the coat/feathers of an animal

b) be carried by the wind

4 The new plants might not get enough light/minerals/water or they would not have enough room to grow.

Fossils (pages 22–23)

1 true: Fossils can be made of minerals or rock, Fossils are still being formed today; false: Fossils are always made from the hard parts of animals, There are only fossils of plants and animals that are extinct. (2 marks for all correct answers, 1 mark for three correct answers)

2 decay/rot away; rivers/lakes/sea/water (both required for 1 mark)

3 two from the following: what colour its fur/feathers/skin/eyes were; what it smelt like; where it laid its eggs; how it looked after its young; how it found a mate

4 a) The mud dried out and the footprint then became covered with more layers of sand or mud, which became compressed and eventually turned to rock.

b) The size/shape of its foot; or whether it had toe nails; or how it moved.

c) A track or trail made by the animal, e.g. by its tail; a burrow made by an animal.

Solids, liquids and gases (pages 24–25)

1 solid: holds its shape, can be cut or shaped, can be poured

liquid: changes shape depending on the container, can be poured

gas: is easily squashed, fills any container it is in; can be poured (e.g. pouring carbon dioxide into tank with candles in to extinguish them) (2 marks for all correct answers; 1 mark for 5–6 correct answers)

2 evaporation; condensation

3 Water boils at 100°C but it can evaporate at any temperature below and up to this temperature.

4 a) 15, 16 or 17

b) The more salt she uses the quicker the ice cream freezes or the less salt she uses the slower the ice cream freezes.

c) a reversible change

5 a) by heating it

b) Because you would not be able to reach the required melting point temperature with conventional heat sources.

The water cycle (pages 26–27)

1 1 evaporates; 2 cools; 3 condenses; 4 forms clouds; 5 falls to Earth's surface; 6 returns to rivers and seas

2 Three of the following: rain, hail, sleet, snow

3 a)

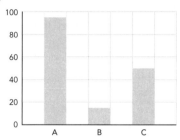

b) The greater the surface area the quicker water evaporates; or the smaller the surface area the slower water evaporates.

c) When there is a larger surface area there is a bigger area for the water particles to evaporate from.

Reversible changes (pages 28–29)

1 true: You can make a material dissolve quicker by stirring, When a material dissolves in a liquid it makes a solution, Dissolving is a reversible change; false: Solutions are always colourless, If a material dissolves you can dissolve any amount of it in the liquid. (2 marks for five correct answers, 1 mark for four correct answers)

2 a) cup/beaker/container, water, different types of sugar, stopwatch/timer

b) each amount of sugar; the temperature of the water

c) to check their results/make sure they have not made any mistakes in their timings

d) the smaller the grain the quicker it dissolves; or the larger the grain the slower it dissolves

3 Filter to get a mixture of flour and iron filings back; Use a magnet to separate the flour and iron filings; Heat the salt solution to evaporate the water and get the salt back. (2 marks for three correct answers, 1 mark for two correct answers)

Irreversible changes (pages 30–31)

1 tick: You can never get the original materials back.

2 you cannot get the wax back once it has changed to a gas

3 The metal changes and often disintegrates and you cannot get the original back.

4 gas/carbon dioxide; vinegar; an irreversible

5 a) Solid butter: reversible

Raw beaten egg: irreversible

Cake mixture: irreversible (all three required for 2 marks)

b) A suitable material, e.g. ice, with columns filled in correctly

Properties and uses of materials (pages 32–33)

1 tick: absorbent, rigid, transparent

2 a) felt: 15; fleece: 21; wool: 25

b) He is not correct. The felt will keep him warmest because the temperature drops less.

3 He could repeat his test in case he has made any mistakes in his measuring.

4 A suitable investigation described to find out about a different property, e.g. absorbency.

Conductors and switches (pages 34–35)

1 true: A switch can be used to complete a circuit, A switch can be used to break a circuit, It doesn't matter where you put a switch in a simple circuit; false: Switches can be made completely from plastic, A light switch has a plastic cover because plastic conducts electricity. (2 marks for five correct answers, 1 mark for four correct answers)

2 E.g. a drill or lawnmower to prevent you getting injured if you slipped or fell.

3 not glow; the plastic straw is an insulator/electricity will not flow through the plastic straw

Changing circuits (pages 36–37)

1 a)

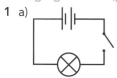

b) tick: Add another cell.

2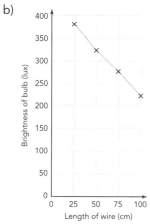

3 a) Add another cell.

b) Count how many times the roundabout spins in half a minute. Add another cell and count again.

c) Change the wires over on the motor or on the cell.

4 a) answer between 215 and 235

b)

(graph: Brightness of bulb (lux) on y-axis from 0 to 400, Length of wire (cm) on x-axis from 0 to 100, with plotted points descending from about 380 at 25 cm to about 220 at 100 cm)

c) The longer the wire, the duller the bulb; or the shorter the wire, the brighter the bulb.

Gravity and resistance (pages 38–39)

1 When two solids rub together – friction; When a solid falls to the ground – gravity; When a solid moves through air – air resistance; When a solid moves through a liquid – water resistance

2 a) scissors 3.0 to 4.8; stone 7 to 10; units, newtons/N added

b) a newton meter or force meter

c) the water pushes up against the objects/upthrust

3 a) gravity; air resistance; friction

b) She could wear tighter-fitting clothes/crouch more over the handlebars/use smoother tyres.

Mechanisms (pages 40–41)

1 true: A lever can use a small amount of force to lift a heavier weight, Gears can be used to change the direction of something that is rotating, Gears have cogs; false: If you use two pulleys to lift an object, you need to use twice as much force, A seesaw does not have a pivot point. (2 marks for five correct answers, 1 mark for four correct answers)

2 a) 1 pivot; 2 pulley (1 mark each)

b) the crane does not tip over/to balance the load

3 a) pan 1

b) Move the pivot towards pan 1.

How we see (pages 42–43)

1 tick: Light travels from the light source, bounces off the object and then goes into our eyes.

2 the light from a vehicle behind bounces off the reflector and back towards the car.

3 a) Light travels in straight lines and cannot bend around a corner.

b) Arrows could be drawn in the opposite direction.

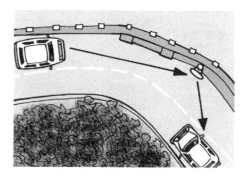

Shadows (pages 44–45)

1 true: Translucent objects make shadows, Shadows move if the object making the shadow moves, The angle of the light source can affect the length of a shadow; false: Only opaque objects make shadows, All shadows are as dark as each other (2 marks for five correct answers, 1 mark for four correct answers)

2 Light travels in straight lines so is blocked by all parts of the child's head. The light cannot bend around the child so the shadow is the same shape. (A simple ray diagram should be drawn to demonstrate this effect, with straight lines drawn from the projector, past the head and onto the wall.)

3 a) 41 cm (accept 40 and 42)

b) The further the book is from the wall, the larger the shadow/the nearer the book is to the wall, the smaller the shadow.

Pitch and volume (pages 46–47)

1 higher: Playing a thinner string, Putting your finger on the string, Making the string tighter

lower: Making the string looser, Playing a thicker string

2 a) For example, make a sound (e.g ring a bell) and use a datalogger to measure how loud it is at different distances.

b) They might have measured different distances or they might not have measured the distances accurately.

3 The less water the higher the note; or the more water the lower the note.

4 a) small tuning folk ticked
b) There is less metal to vibrate so the note is higher.

Our Solar System (pages 48–49)

1 true: The planets orbit the Sun in the same direction, The Earth orbits the Sun; false: The Solar System is made up of the Sun and all the stars in our galaxy, The Moon travels around the Earth once in 24 hours, It takes 356 days for the Earth to orbit the Sun (2 marks for five correct answers, 1 mark for four correct answers)

2 The nearer it is to the Sun, the shorter the time it takes / the further it is from the Sun, the longer it takes.

3 a) 28 days
b) It gets smaller until it disappears and then reappears and gets bigger again / it changes shape every time it appears in the sky.

4 The Sun is huge compared to the planets and the distances are enormous and so it would be difficult to make a model to scale.

5 light; the light from the Sun is reflected from it

Day and night (pages 50–51)

1 tick: The Earth spins on its axis.

2 east; higher; lower

3 When the Sun is low in the sky (early in the day), the shadows are long. When the Sun is high in the sky in the middle of the day, the shadows are short. They get longer as the Sun then gets lower in the sky again.

4 a) Time added to y axis and units written on line.
b) 11:50 to 12:20 (or 12:50 to 13:20 BST)
c) The shadows are longest first thing in the morning, they get shorter until midday and then get longer again.